An Official Document of

The Mystical Order
of the
Nazarene

Liber Sancti Reintegrati Rosarii

Healing the Rose Tree

Elder Zimriah Ex LUX Aeturnus

"Jesus and Mary Magdalene", Kilmore Church, Dervaig, Isle of Mull, Scotland (1904)

Dedicated to:

My mother, father, and siblings – the lessons I learned from you made me who I am today.

My husband - your Love and patience made this possible.

My friends who have been "A Voice In The Wilderness", and whose humility is so great they would not stand for me to name them here.

Preface

Before I explain where this book came from or how it came out of me, I must first praise the One I received it from.

All glory to the Father, Mother, the One Who Is All and only known in silence.

The countenance of my God is all good even when the One only has fury.

Blessed are Your gifts and the Light that shines upon me.

When I am hungry, You provide a feast.

When I am thirsty, You provide an overflowing fountain.

When my lamp shines dimly, You provide the purest oil.

All glory to You, my God.

All glory to You, my God

All glory to You.

When I began writing this book because the Holy Spirit came over me in the form of a torrent of restless energy and ceaseless mental prayers. The most sleep I got within four days was twelve hours. I needed no coffee, no energy drinks, and nothing close to being a stimulant. As I write this preface, the Spirit has left me, yet I can still feel its presence permeating all things. I write this now only as a witness to

God's profound power.

Pieces of this book were already written, such as the alternative utility of the Rosary in the in chapter sixteen. Still, most of this Work was authored in the state of being empowered by the Holy Spirit. It is hard to express what it felt like. Boundless energy, inability to sleep, sometimes pain and aches in my head, the need to write, unfettered focus, and words just coming to my mind. The trances I would go through from lack of sleep had me automatically write. I would just look up at the screen in moments of what I could best call a micro nap and see that I had written a paragraph that was not written before my trance.

I have had similar experiences leading to the founding of The Mystical Order of the Nazarene, but nothing like this. Even so, I think it relates to the Work of the Order. For context, The Mystical Order of the Nazarene (The MON) is an initiatic Esoteric Christian Order focused on studying, practicing, and advancing humanity and the mystical & magical sciences. I founded the Order in 2020 on the Summer Solstice. The system uses techniques such as meditation, contemplation, breathing exercises, Bible study, ritual Work such as theurgy and thaumaturgy, and a few other mystical and magical practices. This is all to better understand God and us for positive self-development.

Since this book and Rosary, through the Order's techniques, came to me in such a manner, they have been adopted as an essential practice of the Order's teachings. The Holy Reintegrated Rosary, if appropriately utilized, can initiate you into several levels of the energetic current the Order draws from. There would be knowledge gaps, but this Rosary is a sound basis for several techniques used by The MON. Anyone interested in joining the Order should start with this humble practice.

Even though the Rosary is now standard practice for this organization, I believe that this new Rosary marks a change in the spirituality and consciousness of humanity. We learn to see and understand symbols in new ways. We are open to new ideas and accept that some good ideas have been suppressed. We are becoming more discerning of our leadership as nations. Many say these are dark times, but in reality, these times are a time of revelation. It only seems darker now because the world's corruption is being revealed.

The same that says we are in a time of darkness also says we are amid the Kali Yuga (a time of great destruction and ignorance), but this just highlights how wrong they are. According to the Vedic tradition, we are within the Dvapara Yuga, a time of uncovering and revealing corruption. We are literally within a time of the cycle where our actions will echo out into the Golden Age a few thousand years ahead of us. It only makes sense that we would see such dark things but take heart and know that we are making our way toward the Light.

That is another thing. What do I mean by Light? Light is a symbol of spiritual knowledge or enlightenment. It is a positive, benevolent force representing the Divine and/or the higher self. In some traditions, Light is associated with Truth and clarity, as it is believed to illuminate the path to understanding and wisdom. Light is closely tied to spiritual growth and attaining higher states of consciousness. The Light is also closely related to the Neshamah or Kundalini Shakti.

Neshamah is a Hebrew term often translated as "soul"

or "breath of life," It is a concept central to many Jewish mystical traditions. Kundalini, on the other hand, is a Hindu term that refers to the spiritual energy that is said to reside at the base of the spine. Both are the same. They are the source of all spiritual power. They are often associated with the awakening of the chakras and the attainment of higher states of consciousness. Within the tradition of The Mystical Order of the Nazarene believe these concepts are syncretic with little difference in the two concepts. This is why the Holy Reintegrated Rosary works with the chakras or what we call lamps.

Much propaganda is made to keep you from working with the "sleeping serpent," but this just goes with the territory. Churches who reject any form of "Gnosticism" find it threatening that any individual part of us works in a mystical way classifying it as magick. This is like the new age types who believe that all magical happening is you and that you are a part of oneness with no hierarchy or more extraordinary spiritual being. In reality, the Truth is found somewhere in the middle. There are mystical parts of our nature that interacts with God. We have our power amplified by working with the One. We are all separate but one, yet even into eternity, we will still have an individuated and united consciousness.

When we let go of the arrogance of thinking we know it all and allow God to inform us, we can see the Truth behind most ideas. I hope this clarifies what may be missing from this book and add some context that may not have reached you without this supplemental writing. May God bless you, your kin, and the rest of humanity age after age for all eternity.

-Elder Zimriah Ex LUX Aeturnus

"Call to me, and I will answer you and will tell you great and hidden things that you have not known."

~ Jeremiah 33:3

Chapter One: Healing the Rose Tree

"A Rose Garden" by Gustave Bienvetu (1902)

y brothers and sisters, those who seek the Truth in every facet of reality, it is with great joy that I can share these "secrets" with you. As secrets go, nothing is genuinely secret; some things are just hidden from us until we seek them out. Here you are seeking, and I am willing to give and not hide away the beautiful Truth before you: a Rose Tree that I have nursed to good health so that the Light may shine from it.

This book is for the sake of clarity and Wisdom. The

book of Luke warns, "no one after lighting a lamp puts it in a cellar or under a bushel basket; rather, one puts it on the lampstand so that those who enter may see the Light. Your eye is the lamp of your body. If your eye is healthy, your whole body is full of Light, but if it is unhealthy, your body is full of darkness. Therefore, consider whether the Light in you is not darkness. But if your whole body is full of Light, with no part of it in darkness, it will be as full of Light as when a lamp gives you light with its rays" (Luke 11:33-36).

Making the body healthy means removing every malignancy, which begins with the knowledge you know and starts in your mind. This Rose Tree, this Rosary, is a lamp I have lit for you to share with you for the increase of your Light. We are in a time where everything hidden is to be revealed in what some call the Age of Aquarius. The disclosure of every secret is expressed in Luke 8:17, "for nothing is hidden that will not be disclosed, nor is anything secret that will not become known and come to light."

The Rosary was/is a fantastic innovation in Christianity's practices and is self-evident in its perpetuation.

The founder of the Rosary is unknown. However, the desert mothers and fathers of the early Church utilized knotted rope to keep count of their prayers and meditations, highlighting how ancient this tradition truly is. A beautiful and mystical story depicts the prayer rope becoming the Rosary through St. Dominick, who reported receiving instructions in making the prayer beads in a vision of the Virgin Mary. This Rosary, as we know it now, became a typical tradition under the rule of Pope Pius V.

It is unknown what this practice may have looked like in the earliest days of Christianity. Yet, the Rosary's utility of stringed beads echoes throughout the world's spiritual practices, such as Buddhism, Islam, Sikhism, Hinduism, and much more. With most religions being syncretic, it points to an underlying ancient tradition from which all these religions were devised. Nevertheless, this tradition is now lost to us. In this ancient practice, meditation was a core piece where the practitioner would develop their ability to focus and depth of awareness, creating emotional calm and stability. This book is not about unveiling this hidden tradition but expressing the Christian tradition neglected in the Rosary.

At a point where it seemed the Sacred Feminine was to be wiped clean from the Christian tradition, a truly Divine intervention took place. A thousand years after the passing of Jesus, a group within the Church preserved the Divine Feminine through the "Hail Mary." This prayer became one of the fondest prayers among the Catholics and became a central prayer within the Rosary. In Truth, before the founding of Catholicism, the Divine Feminine was not always so dissociated nor esoteric in the case of the Holy Spirit. Truthfully, the Holy Spirit is recognized as a feminine aspect of the Trinity. Yet, most people would not realize this due to language barriers.

The Truth about the Messiah has been held in the hands of a select few for some time now. Most of these few will be ignorant of the whole story or not see how the Church was led astray by Roman rule. It is my ego and the frustration I empathize with coming from the collection of humanity that I wish to recount the sins of the successors of Peter, Christ's rock. But that is not the Way. The Light of Truth shall always prevail in the face of darkness.

I have written this to refresh a withering rose. I do this to follow the commandment, "let us crown ourselves with rosebuds before they wither" (Wisdom of Solomon 2:8). These buds of roses are Light, and that Light is in the shape of a crown. Kether, as the Hebrew tradition calls it. The same Light that roared out of the burning bush and exclaimed, "אֶהְיֶה אֲשֶׁר אֶהְיֶה" (Ehyeh Asher Ehyeh: I am that I am). This Light of God shines brighter than it ever has before.

Beginning the rectification through God's faithful and mighty Love, I reveal a truth hidden for some time. Nonetheless, it has risen from the same sands our Jesus walked. Christians recognized the divine feminine under the name of Sophia, meaning Wisdom or internal understanding, our Lady Mary Magdalene. She was a counterpart, consort to the Logos meaning the Word of God, and Logic, Lord Jesus. Unified, they made the true wholeness of the tradition that we call Christianity today, yet what we have now is a broken tradition –half of an ancient truth. Though it may seem heretical, at one point, this was not designated as such until the Roman Empire infiltrated the Church all those years ago.

When this happened, a whole group of people who were part of the faith was shunned and demonized. This group was called Christians, but after the demonization, propagandists called them Gnostics - as they are today. Apologists who continue to ignore these ostracized Christians throw many reasons around why the "Gnostics" were rejected, but only one reason makes sense. Only one thing would make the Empire force these Christians out, fear of the power behind them. Nevertheless, the "Gnostics" and Christians disagreed entirely on recognized canon; they shared their faith, debated, and were abused by the Empire all the same as Christians. The Christians whose teachings were authorized accepted this shunning of their brothers and sisters only because it was a reprieve from their government's abuse. But this book is not a sorrowful lesson in history. It is Good News.

The Sacred Union (in Greek, the term would be Hieros Gamos: ἱερός γάμος) of Jesus and Mary Magdalene is a belief held by individuals and spiritual traditions still today.

However, it is not a widely accepted doctrine within mainstream Christianity still. Jesus and Mary Magdalene were married or had a romantic and spiritual relationship. Their union was a sacred and vital part of Jesus' ministry and teachings as Logos. Those who believe in the Sacred Union of Jesus and Mary Magdalene often argue that the marriage of Jesus and Mary Magdalene is mentioned or hinted at in the Gospels. Yet a lot of the information is lost to time, for now.

Some proponents of this belief argue that Jesus and Mary Magdalene were married in a ceremony similar to traditional Jewish weddings and that their union was a sacred and holy bond. Many say that Jesus' marriage to Mary Magdalene symbolized his commitment to Love and compassion and was essential to his message of salvation and redemption. Mary Magdalene, being Sophia, continued the ministry as the Sophian tradition after being rejected by Peter, according to *The Gospel of Mary Magdalene*.

This book's purpose is not to argue the finer points proving Jesus and Mary Magdalene's Hieros Gamos. Here is a list of missing gospels that may dispel any doubt about the

Sacred Union in the discerning reader:

> ✝ *The Gospel According to Mary Magdalene*
>
> ✝ *The Gospel of Philip*
>
> ✝ *Gospel of St. Thomas*
>
> ✝ *The Lost Gospel* by Simcha Jacobovic

I feel a sense of duty, an urgency to be a light unto my brothers and sisters. There is a passion within me not to regulate nor give definitive answers as to how one should pray, the Order of those prayers, and the number of recitations. I am moved by the Spirit to reveal an ancient Christian practice almost lost to us. This rejuvenated Rose Tree is an example of what that practice could have looked like if only it had been nurtured and passed down, not suppressed.

The Holy Reintegrated Rosary is a restoration of the esoteric and the exoteric, Gnostic tradition with Orthodoxy and the mystical with the mundane. It is why this Rosary is called the Holy Reintegrated Rosary. The Rosary's original purpose was to rectify some ideological changes in Roman Christianity. However, it falls short of the spiritual Truth of the wholeness of the tradition. If Catholic means a universal Christianity, then why leave out any part?

Again, I want to make it abundantly clear that I, Elder Zimriah, and the Mystical Order of the Nazarene do not seek to attack nor disparage our Catholic brothers and sisters in Christ. It is not the Way, and it is not our personal goal. Since the Roman Empire, later becoming the Holy See, hiding the Truth for so long, the exposure of it can feel like a wound to the ego. Primarily if we identify with those that hid the fact in the first place. However, you who innocently feel attacked should know it is not your fault what evils have happened. You are not the deceivers. You are our brothers and sisters. Even if you do not accept this ancient Truth, that is fine. It is also not our goal to start a crusade and force you to drink from this fount of Wisdom. It is every man and woman's prerogative to believe as they wish.

The Holy Reintegrated Rosary revitalizes this sacred Rose Tree passed down to us for centuries. It is not the first reformation of the Rosary, and it will not be the last. This Rosary that I put forward as a working basis for true Gnostic

Christianity. The mission of this Order, The Mystical Order of the Nazarene, makes it a solemn duty to reformulate the Christian tradition so that it puts it back on track from before the Nicaean Councils. The suppression of knowledge makes the Truth impossible to find. May the Holy Reintegrated Rosary be a Light of Truth shining through the darkness of ignorance that surrounds this sacred tradition.

Chapter Two: The Holy Reintegrated Rosary

As was stated before, the Rosary's creation is mostly unknown to most, and most legends give a hyper-mystical vision of how it came to be. In reality, the Rosary's conception came about through a combination of esoteric knowledge and a spiritual science called theurgy. Theurgy is a practice that strives to elevate the psyche into higher frequency worlds/realms/dimensions, causing change within the self and sometimes outside oneself with or without the aid of the Divine. The name Rosary (meaning crown or garland or ring of roses) hints at this esoteric nature. The mystical meaning of the rose is Light or, more specifically, the Light within or enlightenment. This reveals the function of the Rosary, to become enlightened by meditating on the narrative of Jesus's life. Doing this all the while praying places the mind in a higher frequency of thinking.

The formulation of the Holy Reintegrated Rosary is highly symbolic. The colors, stone type, prayers, number of beads, mysteries, and links that separate the different prayers are wholly unique from the Catholic Rosary. An explanation of the new Rosary's blessings is in chapters four through six. For now, we will go over the symbolic meaning of the components of this profound and refreshed Rosary. I will not demystify every mystical component of the Holy Reintegrated Rosary in this book. A part of the spiritual experience is to understand these symbols. The Mystical Order of the Nazarene must respect these self-discovered revelations since the Holy Reintegrated Rosary is an important teaching tool.

Esoteric Symbols within the Holy Reintegrated Rosary

The Holy Reintegrated Rosary (HRR) comprises sixty-five beads and consists of twelve prayers: seven Archangel prayers, "The Emanator's prayer," "Veni Creator Spiritus," "Hail Mary Magdalene," "The Jesus Prayer," and "The Prayer of the Sacred Union." The number of beads represents the ten sefirot of the Kabbalistic Tree of Life, including the hidden sefirah (65 beads = 6 + 5 = 11 sefirot). All colors and stone types are pertinent as they represent multiple spiritual truths.

The first seven beads correspond with seven angels, seven planets, and the seven energetic centers of the body recognized as lamps in Revelation and chakras in Tantric Hinduism. The color of the beads also corresponds to the planets and are placed on the Rosary from the bottom up Saturn, Jupiter, Mars, Venus, Mercury, Luna, and Sol. The next set of ten beads marks the beginning of the five decades representing the mysteries chosen as the focus of your meditation. Each black and white bead of the decades represents God's wholeness and corresponds to the sefirot of the Tree of Life without the hidden sefirah. These beads are for the Emanator's Prayer, a reinterpretation of the Lord's Prayer.

Two beads follow the ten beads beginning the decades, representing Jesus and Mary Magdalene. The red bead correspondent to Jesus, representing his sacrifice, the Light of his knowledge is the Logos of God, and the color corresponds to Mars. The turquoise bead represents Mary Magdalene. The color blends with Her connection to Heaven and Earth, her power as Sophia of God, and Venus. I have revealed enough of the color correspondence of the beads.

The two charms that adorn the HRR represent many truths yet are relatively recognizable to most. A cross that the Mystical Order of the Nazarene calls the Sign of the New Covenant and a hexagram or what some would identify as דָּוִד מָגֵן (Magen David, which translates to the Shield of David). The Sign of the Covenant is a cross with a pentacle resting at the center of the cross-section. This symbol has a similar meaning to the Rosy Cross: life, death, sacrifice, the Light within physical matter, the spiritual origins of the world, and a sign of blooming enlightenment through the balancing of the four elements (air, fire, water, and earth). This elemental nature of the cross is the esoteric reasoning for why Christians cross themselves with the cross –creating internal balance and rectification.

The pentagram within the pentacle represents the four elements ruled by spirit. A superficial interpretation of the pentagram is the 5 wounds Jesus received during the crucifixion process. More esoterically, it means the evolution of rule from Yahweh to the law of Yahoshuah (the Hebrew name of Jesus). The Hebrew spelling of Jesus fits perfectly within the pentagram representing a myriad of ideas, such as the power of spirit over the four elements. The circle around the pentagram makes it a pentacle allowing it to work as a talisman holding in energy and amplifying it. Your prayers and what you say as your hand touches the cross give it a specific resonance

The Magen David is a symbol the Israelites adopted to represent their faith and nation. Even though the hexagram is a much more ancient symbol (as all signs are, really). One meaning of the hexagram represents the union of alchemical water and fire or the balancing of equally opposite forces. Ultimately that would mean balancing emotional forces within – a collaboration of the feminine and masculine energy within. This meaning explains why the Hebrews chose the hexagram as the Shield of David. The first commandment to the Hebrews was to "be fruitful and multiply" (Genesis 1:28).

The intersecting triangles are recognized to have gendered meanings. The triangle pointing up is masculine, and the triangle pointing down is feminine; thus, it represents the Sacred Union of man and woman, which bears children. As a tantric symbol, the intersecting triangles represent the act of transmuting sexual energy. This is a High Mystery within The Mystical Order of the Nazarene. The prayer associated with this symbol in this Rosary indeed echoes these concepts.

Metaphysical Qualities of the Stone Beads

The type of stone utilized for each bead is pertinent, having its intangible quality. Each stone aids in the resonance of the specific prayers. The attributes appropriately respond to the correspondent ideas in the symbolism of the different parts of the Rosary outlined before. For example, the first seven stones represent the seven lamps across the body as depicted in Revelation 1:12-13. The first stone of the seven represents the first lamp or chakra corresponding to the planet Saturn. When this lamp becomes corrupt, fear and neurosis develop; thus, the best choice is onyx for its strength, protection, and willpower. The black color of the stone also corresponds with the planet Saturn making this the perfect stone.

The prayers mention the corresponding planets for each bead representing the lamps of the spirit body, leaving no need to list them in the stone description. Below is a list of qualities of each stone used in the Rosary:

Black Onyx—The onyx is a stone that offers its bearer sensations of protection, willpower, focus, and strength. Many believe that the onyx drives motivation and continuously pushes you forward.

Blue Spot Jasper—This stone bears stable grounding and substantial healing properties. Blue spot jasper is known to emit constant and slow energy to allow you to be in your physical self. The stone brings calmness, builds inner strength, and promotes courage. Jasper aids in balancing sexual energy. In the ancient world, Jasper was used to boost libido.

Carnelian—Carnelian captivates in much the same way that the flash of a fiery sunset or the first blaze of autumnal brilliance does. It symbolizes bold energy, warmth, and joy that empowers and stimulates. Carnelian is also known to enhance the power of other stones, giving holders a boost in their passions.

Green Aventurine—Green Aventurine is a great stabilizer, uniting the logical, emotional, material, and light bodies in bringing one back into a natural rhythm. It dissolves negativity and balances the masculine and feminine energies, enabling one to live within the heart space. This stone makes one feel optimistic and want positive and constructive action.

Woodgrain Jasper—woodgrain jasper is believed to comprise an ability to establish a bond between the wearer and their innate Love for nature. This stone is also considered a respectful stone that encourages holders to look at their environment and nature serenely. The stone creates natural communication coming from the core of the individual.

Amethyst—The influence that Amethyst can have on its surroundings dates at least as far back as Ancient Greece. It brings clarity of mind, enhances intuition, and enhances thought processing. Amethyst also allows the holder to go deeper into meditative states of mind.

Yellow Jade - is said to be a Wisdom stone, helping users learn from their experiences and gain self-confidence. Yellow as a color also symbolizes warmth and joy. Said to bring good fortune and luck. It is almost always associated with the Sun, making Yellow Jade a stone of confidence.

White Howlite—Formulates ambitions and aids in achieving them. Howlite improves memory, increases the desire for knowledge, teaches patience, and helps eliminate anger, pain, and stress. A soothing stone, Howlite calms communication, facilitates awareness, and encourages emotional manifestation.

Turquoise—a stone of purification. Turquoise dispels negative energy and is worn to protect against outside influences, promotes self-realization, and assists creative problem-solving. It is a representation of friendship and stimulates compassion. Turquoise is closely associated with Wisdom and inner knowledge. Many believe the stone has healing properties. It is closely related to the lamp of the heart or heart chakra.

Red Tiger's Eye—This will ensure you have all the skills you need to survive and preserve yourself. These qualities are why Red Tiger's Eye is known as the "survival stone." It helps us reconnect with the essential aspects of our life on this Earth and see where we waste our time and energies. This crystal is also a solid motivational stone used to bring a sense of regularity and calm to your life, even if you juggle too many tasks or ideas.

Chapter Three: How to Pray the Holy Reintegrated Rosary

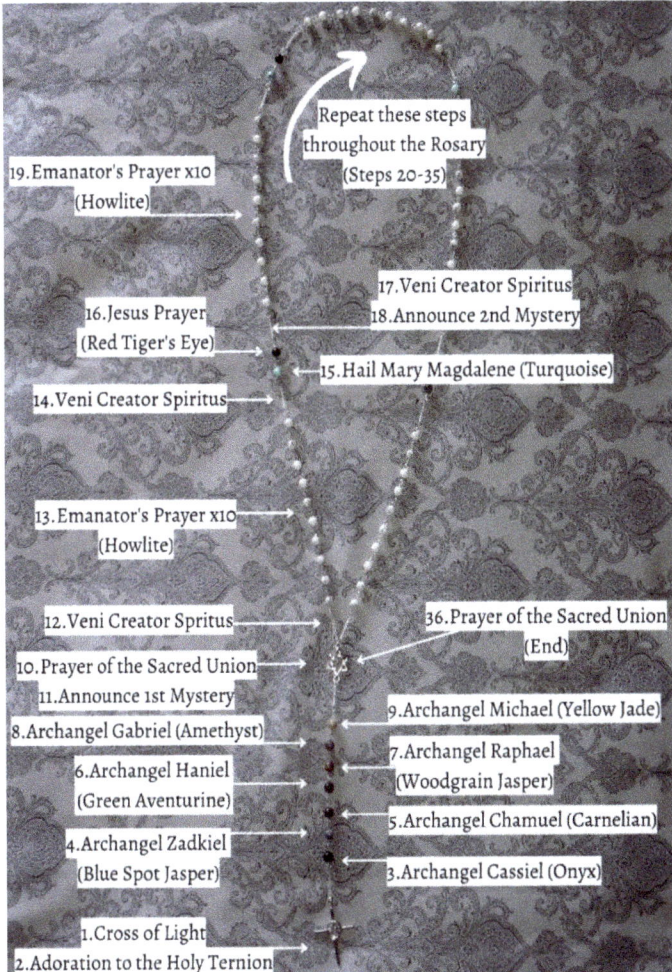

19. Emanator's Prayer x10 (Howlite)

Repeat these steps throughout the Rosary (Steps 20-35)

17. Veni Creator Spiritus
18. Announce 2nd Mystery

16. Jesus Prayer (Red Tiger's Eye)

15. Hail Mary Magdalene (Turquoise)

14. Veni Creator Spiritus

13. Emanator's Prayer x10 (Howlite)

12. Veni Creator Spritus

36. Prayer of the Sacred Union (End)

10. Prayer of the Sacred Union

11. Announce 1st Mystery

9. Archangel Michael (Yellow Jade)

8. Archangel Gabriel (Amethyst)

7. Archangel Raphael (Woodgrain Jasper)

6. Archangel Haniel (Green Aventurine)

5. Archangel Chamuel (Carnelian)

4. Archangel Zadkiel (Blue Spot Jasper)

3. Archangel Cassiel (Onyx)

1. Cross of Light
2. Adoration to the Holy Ternion

A Diagram of the Holy Reintegrated Rosary

The Holy Reintegrated Rosary is a meditative prayer like the Catholic Rosary. Many types of meditation will bring us closer to the Grace of God or the Heart of Grace. However, the Rosary is a reflective practice presented in Romans 12:22, "Do not be conformed to this world, but be transformed by the renewing of your minds, so that you may discern the will of God—what is good and acceptable and perfect is." This is called contemplative meditation. Contemplation meditation seeks to create a direct awareness toward the Divine or consideration of a specific idea, question, or situation to receive insight from the still small voice, inner Wisdom, or the Divine, that transcends the intellect.

This Rosary process allows you to do three things in a circle reflecting on the self through narrative, praying in a chant-like fashion without losing place, and letting you lay your awareness casually on the symbolism of the prayer beads. As you may notice, a lot is going on with how the Rosary operates, but it becomes much more straightforward with practice. I outline the operation of the HRR as a schedule assuming the operator has never meditated before so that anyone of any level can take part.

While working through this schedule, if you choose, I recommend memorizing prayers and learning the meanings of the stones and symbols of the Rosary as you go along. Part of the meditation is to allow these ideas to be points of contemplation. Don't worry or feel pressured to learn it quickly. Just begin where you can and go from there. Eventually, when you go to do the Rosary's entire operation, the repetition and utility of the knowledge will solidify it in your memory. The biggest thing is not to overthink it and realize you will eventually get it. You can commit the Mysteries to memory, but it is unnecessary initially.

Week One - Three

Sit somewhere comfortably, whether in a chair, legs crisscrossed, or whatever makes you feel comfortable and allows you to sit up with your spine as erect and straight as possible. Perform the "Cross of Light" (CoL) and then recite the "Adoration of the Holy Ternion" (AHT).

When you repeat the adoration, hold the cross and beads close to the center of your chest. Close your eyes and check in with your mind. Observe what kind of mood you are in and how you feel. Listen to your environment and notice each sound and where it originates.

Now narrow your focus internally to the breath entering and exiting your nostrils. As you take deep breaths that expand the belly, begin to slow into a rhythm and feel as if the breath is entering and exiting the heart. Smile as naturally as you can with your eyes still closed, and think of something extremely positive that makes you feel Love, appreciation, and gratitude. Whatever it may be, make sure it is solid and positive and allow it to radiate through your whole being. Do this for ten minutes. If you notice your awareness moves from focusing on the breath and these feelings, bring it gently back into your attention of these things and praise yourself for refocusing. End the session by kissing the cross. Within the three weeks, adding one and a half minutes every three days is pertinent.

Week Four – Six

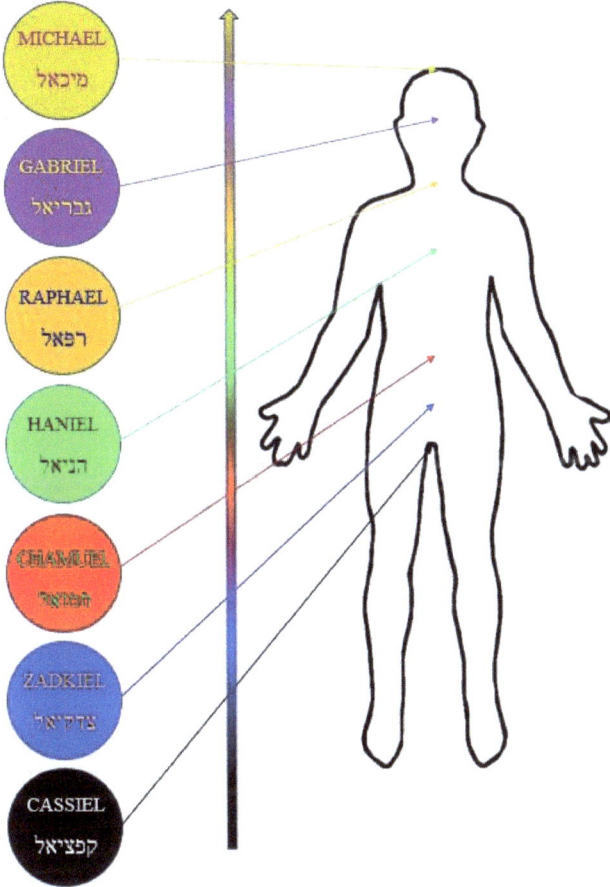

A diagram of the Lamps and corresponding Archangels.

Begin as you did before: sit comfortably with your

spine as erect as possible, perform and recite the CoL and

AHT, check in with your mind, and bring your awareness to the breath flowing through the heart and the positive emotion while smiling. When you feel ready, place your attention on the beads in your hand. Feel the smoothness. Are the stones cool to the touch or warm? What are some comparisons you can make?

Take a few moments to focus on these things but then sandwich the first bead between the pointer finger and the thumb. Without breaking concentration, take a look at the bead. What color is it? What does this bead represent? Which lamp/chakra does it influence? Where is that on your body? These are the kinds of questions you should be asking yourself. Now recite the prayer related to it. What does the prayer mean to you – how do you connect? Do this for every bead related to the lamps of the body, trying to spend only 3 minutes on each bead. This process should last from twenty-one to twenty-five minutes.

Week Seven – Nine

Follow all of the previous steps you did in all of the

earlier sessions. Some parts of the process should be quicker to activate at this point. When comfortable moving on, follow the path through the rest of the Rosary. Treat each part as you did the first seven beads: touching the bead/charm/chain, asking yourself pertinent questions, and then reciting the prayer corresponding to what you are handling. If you lack awareness of what you are doing, forget something and have to look back at the book, or slip out of your meditative state, do not fret. Compassionately place your awareness where you need it to be and positively acknowledge yourself for getting back on track.

From This Point Forward

At this point, it would be appropriate to add in the mysteries. Follow all previous steps except when you get to the hexagram and announce the Mystery you plan to contemplate. Proceed forward with the prayers but notice that before you start reciting the "Emanator's Prayer" and right after reciting "Veni Creator Spiritus," you announce the decades of the Mystery. There are 5 decades for every set of 10 Howlite beads. When going over the decades and praying with the bead in hand, you should think deeply about the decade you internally announced. Ask yourself similar questions as you did with the beads before. You should also contemplate the connection between the prayer you are reciting, the decade, and how both connect the meaning of the bead itself. How do you relate to it? So on and so forth.

Praying With A Goal In Mind – Supplication

We pray for many reasons: to meditate, to show gratitude, to convey sorrow, to celebrate, to bless, etc. The list of the purposes of prayer could go on page after page. Still, for whatever purpose you decide to pray, emotion will play a significant role if it is not for meditation. True, you want to take on meditation with a positive attitude, a smile from within and out, and positive emotion. Yet, the subject of emotion and the prayer goes deeper than this. The feelings behind your intent make a considerable impact on the effectiveness of your prayers.

Feeling the emotions surrounding your intention is the key to allowing the prayer to be heard by God, or at least for God to act in your favor. John 5:15 states, "and if we know that he hears us in whatever we ask, we know that we have obtained the requests made of him." The question becomes, how do we know? Mark 11:24 makes it even more transparent, "so I tell you, whatever you ask for in prayer, believe that you have received it, and it will be yours."

It is through feeling and emotion that lends the knowing or Gnosis. This is the epitome of faith, us knowing and feeling gratitude toward our intent as if it already happened. Of course, it has more of a process, especially when using a tool like the Rosary to pray. To make this easier to digest, below will be a simple outline of this process:

I. **Feel as if your prayer is already answered** – Whatever it is that you are praying for at the moment, sit down and pray to feel with your heart, mind, and body that it is done. Use your imagination to see how you would feel and celebrate the answered prayer and allow all that flowing from the heart to the mind and then the rest of the body.

II. **Say aloud confidently, "Lord, I come before You to (state intent of the prayer)."** – "Lord, I come before You to heal my knee injury." "Lord, I come before You to receive a monetary raise at work" "Lord, I come before You to mend the relationship between my child and me." Whatever you want from God, say it concisely and to the point.

III. **Pray the Holy Reintegrated Rosary** – This is the time to get lost in your prayers but follow all of the steps of the prayer sequence as you learned it from day one. Pray with all of your heart and mind singularly focused on working as one. You should repeat step two in the places where you would usually announce the mystery before every decade.

IV. **Give thanks to God** – Thank God for fulfilling your prayer. Give Him all of your adoration. You could repeat the "Adoration to the Holy Ternion" if you feel that is sufficient.

V. **Thoroughly seal the prayer** – To lock the prayer correctly, you must reaffirm your faith and trust in God. This would be like the end of the "Emanator's Prayer," but adding the end of the "Cross of Light," "may these words be my nature sealed in trust, faith, and Truth. Forever and ever without end. Amen." If you prefer, instead of saying "forever and ever without end," you can say "L'Olemei Olamim."

A few more things I would like to add. As you will learn from the Mysteries of the Emanator, God enjoys secrecy to a degree; well, humility - to be more exact. The prayer or ritual will not be fulfilled if we perform our rites boastfully or with a sense of arrogance. To convey this powerful principle, Jesus said, "Beware of practicing your righteousness before others to be seen by them, for then you have no reward from your Father in heaven… And whenever you pray, do not be like the hypocrites, for they love to stand and pray in the synagogues and at the street corners, so that they may be seen by others. Truly I tell you, they have received their reward" (Matthew 6:1, 5). In this case, the attention one receives from one's prayers and rites is the prayer answered. Because of this, God has already acted, not acting any further.

This does not mean we cannot come together, pray, or do rituals. It is said in Matthew 18:20, "for where two or three are gathered in my name, I am there among them." Here we see that even though we are in the presence of others, our prayers, in this case, are amplified. The key is that we do not gather out of the motivation of an arrogant ego. We should come together in pursuit of connecting with God to fulfill an intent in complete care and faith in one another and God.

How Meditation And Prayer Affect Us

There are some things I would like to highlight to help dispel myths and to help you get the most out of this practice. It is commonly believed that meditation should wipe your mind clear of thought during training, but this is not necessarily true. I call it training on purpose. The mind will always try to jump from one subject of focus to the next, which is what you are trying to keep from happening. Essentially it is a training in focus. Do not be afraid to be "bad" at meditation because that is the training aspect of it, refocusing. You should allow the mind to flow. Naturally, become aware of the slip of focus, and then congratulate yourself for refocusing during your sessions (this last step cannot be missed).

As your relationship with the Rosary and God grows through prayers and devotions, new questions and understanding of what you are doing and why you are doing it are revealed. This is expanding the mind and consciousness and coming into the Heart of Grace. This Heart of Grace is exemplified in Hebrews 13:9, "do not be carried away by all kinds of strange teachings, for it is good for the heart to be strengthened by grace, not by regulations about food, which have not benefited those who observe them." This verse teaches us that no number of human-made laws can bring forth the miracles formed by God's Grace.

Grace is the free, unearned gift of heavenly favor in the redemption of sinners and the deific influence operating in individuals for their restoration and consecration. Through meditation, we realize that God's Agape or Love is unconditional. God affords this Grace to us, and then we eventually afford our Grace to others, becoming an expression of Agape. This process is called coming into the Heart of Grace. In the Heart of Grace, no fear or amount of suffering can shake you.

Beyond coming into the Heart of Grace, here is a short list of benefits that you will gain from this contemplation meditation:

† Increased positive mood.

† Improved concentration and meta-awareness (a purposeful focus on how you are developing and maintaining your situational awareness).

† Sustained motivation and less procrastination.

† Improved immune function.

† Less anxiety and depression.

† Slower aging.

† Remarkable synchronicities (events that seem related to each other and/or related to a practice one performs in some manner, yet there is no discernable proof of connection to be evident to those outside the experience).

The prayers will begin to transform your mind and brain even. Reshaping and creating new neural pathways. Exciting the brain in ways that can only be recreated with substances, but luckily prayer and meditation do not have such adverse secondary effects as these substances will. It is common knowledge now that a meditative and spiritual practice alleviates the cravings related to addiction and boosts the motivation to want to stay free from substance abuse. The motivation factor created by meditation helps all people in all facets of life. Motivation is established through the ability to focus on one objective at a time for more extended periods than you would without meditation.

Note On The Prayers In The Next Few Chapters

Most of these prayers that will be found in this book are wholly unique, yet some of them may sound familiar. The nature of the beliefs and knowledge surrounding the HRR called for creating new prayers and reinterpretations of others. You could develop your prayers for the Rosary, which would be recommended. As stated before, your emotions and connections to the words are vital. This is why prayers have been reinterpreted so that a complete understanding of the prayer is more feasible.

If you decide to formulate your prayers, make sure you understand what the prayer is conveying to form a new prayer with the same intent. Also, note that some words in some of these prayers are in all capital letters. Capitalizing every letter of a word means singing the word or vibrating it so that the body vibrates with the resonance of the sound. This singing and vibrating of words are an expression of frequency to further the alignment of the mind, body, and spirit.

Chapter Four: Opening Prayers

The Cross of Light is an interesting prayer. Many Christian denominations cross themselves before prayer, after, when they enter a church, and it is called making the Sign of the Cross. While making the Sign of the Cross, it is traditional to say, "In the name of the Father, the Son, and the Holy Spirit." No one asks themselves who passed down this practice. Was it the clergy? Or was it Jesus himself? From talking to many people across many Christian denominations, they tend to assume the latter oddly enough. That is when I usually ask if it was before or after the crucifixion – minds tend to wander after I ask that question.

Not many tend to think too deeply about Jesus' Hebrew faith. Yet, if they did, they would probably discover that Jesus most likely studied and practiced Kabbalah. Kabbalah is a school of thought in Jewish mysticism that explores the nature of God, the universe, and humanity's role. It originated in ancient Judaism and is considered a mystical tradition that focuses on understanding the spiritual realm and how it relates to the physical world. Kabbalah often involves the study of various texts, including the Torah and the Zohar, and using meditation and other spiritual practices to gain deeper insights into the nature of God and the universe.

Why is this pertinent? Let us look at the end of the common interpretation of the Lord's prayer, "For there is the Kingdom, the power and the glory, forever and ever. Amen." This phrase within the prayer alone is highly Kabbalistic. Kingdom in Hebrew is roughly translated to Mamlakha or Malkuth, power is translated as Gevurah, and glory would be Gedulah or Chesed. These are also names of components (called sefirot or emanations) of an important symbol within Kabbalah, the Etz Chaim (the Tree of Life). Even saying "for Thine," you are referring to the highest of the sefirot, Kether, which I wrote about in the first chapter. "Forever and ever" refers to the equilibrator of the sefirot called Tiphareth.

When you combine the Sign of the Cross with Kabbalistic concepts, you get the Qabalistic Cross, a ritual gesture used in western magic. The term magic, I recognize, is deemed heretical in most Christian denominations. Still, there are a lot of misnomers of what constitutes magic and why it was considered evil. I recommend the book *Magic in Christianity: From Jesus to the Gnostics* by Robert Conner for a detailed deep dive into the subject. The difference in the spelling of Kabbalah connotes a different branch of the tradition.

The Qabalistic Cross is a way of attuning oneself to the energies of the Tree of Life, a key concept in Qabalistic philosophy. The gesture involves touching the forehead, then the breast, then the right and left shoulders, and finally, the feet while reciting specific divine names. Qabalistic philosophy sees this as aligning the mind and body with the Divine and bringing Light into the physical realm. Also, the mind and body are rectified by balancing the philosophical elements.

The Adoration to the Holy Ternion is a play on a prayer found in the Hermetic book called *The Corpus Hermeticum,* said to be written by Hermes Trismegistus. In this adoration, we give all of the glory to the different aspects of the Holy Trinity/Ternion. The Logos and Sophia are represented as one aspect even though they are two – the revelation of the Sacred Union reveals this Truth. Esoterically you could argue that these three aspects represent the aspects of the mind and brain:

† The Father is symbolized in the cortex and the frontal lobes,

† Logos in the brain stem and parietal lobes,

† Sophia in the cerebellum and occipital lobes,

† Holy Spirit in the basil ganglia and temporal lobes.

It is interesting to note the brain stem and cerebellum are pressed against each other; you could even call it a Sacred Union.

When adding these anatomical aspects into the prayers, it almost seems like a form of self-worship or worship of the human body. It cannot be denied. Our ancestors were fascinated by the human body. They even created temples to be in the body's shape. However, I would argue that this is too simple of an answer that explains away the mystical synchronistic happening of this Truth. The ancient Greeks, called Hermeticists, had several principles they observed in the world, one of which was the Principle of Correspondence. This principle is established on the idea that the lesser parts are equal in some nature to the greater parts. This means that the macrocosm (the universe) and the microcosm (the individual) are interconnected and follow the same laws. This principle is often associated with the idea that everything in the universe is connected, and correspondences exist between different levels of reality. It would only make sense that God and His Wholeness echo throughout all creation.

Cross of Light

(With the cross, touch your forehead.) "Ki Lekha" or "You are"

(Touch below the navel.) "Ha'Mamlakha" or "the Kingdom"

(Touch left shoulder.) "Veh Ha'Gevurah" or "and the Judge"

(Touch right shoulder.) "Veh Ha'Gedulah" or "and the Merciful"

(Hold the cross to your chest.) "L'Olemei Olamim" or "Forever and ever without end."

(Kiss the cross at the center.) "Amen"

"Trinity of Salerno" by Jakob Beohme

Adoration to the Holy Ternion

Glory be to the Father who is only known in silence.

Glory be to Sophia and Logos, who redeem the whole world.

Glory be to the Holy Spirit, who enlightens a flame in our hearts.

Glory be to the Holy Ternion of Light within the Dark.

Chapter Five: Angelic Prayers

T he angelic prayers presented are a condensed version of a rite within The Mystical Order of the Nazarene called The Lighting of the Seven Lamps. The ritual was inspired by Revelation 1: 12-16, "Then I turned to see whose voice it was that spoke to me, and on turning I saw seven golden lampstands, and in the midst of the lampstands I saw one like the Son of Man, clothed with a long robe and with a golden sash across his chest. His head and his hair were white as white wool, white as snow; his eyes were like a flame of fire; his feet were like burnished bronze, refined as in a furnace, and his voice was like the sound of many waters. In his right hand he held seven stars, and from his mouth came a sharp, two-edged sword, and his face was like the sun shining with full force."

It has been acknowledged in many mystical Christian traditions that John the Elder is seeing Jesus in His Lightbody. The Lightbody is a concept in various spiritual and metaphysical beliefs, which refers to an ethereal, luminous body believed to be the proper form of the physical body. It is said to be made of pure Light and consciousness and is sometimes associated with the aura or the astral body. The Lightbody is considered the vehicle for the soul or higher self and is believed to be a part of an individual's spiritual power and wisdom. In some beliefs, the Lightbody is thought to be the key to spiritual evolution and enlightenment and can be activated or awakened through various spiritual practices.

One of the practices utilized to develop the Lightbody is to meditate and energetically influence seven energy centers across the body, which refers to seven lampstands/lamps. In Tantric Hinduism, these energy centers are called chakras (चक्र: wheel). The lamps are lit by the Light of the Neshamah or Kundalini Shakti for the Tantric Hindus. The angels correspond to a lamp, a planet, and an ancient church. The churches and planetary correspondence also come from the book of Revelation. The angel acts as a guardian for each lamp and church, so in the prayers, we ask that they remove corruptions and replace them with their equal opposite.

Archangel Cassiel Prayer

Archangel Cassiel, guardian of Saturn and the Church of Ephesus, remove neurosis and grant me lucidity. CASSIEL! CASSIEL! CASSIEL!

Archangel Zadkiel Prayer

Archangel Zadkiel, guardian of Jupiter and the Church of Smyrna, remove guilt and grant me the ability to forgive. ZADKIEL! ZADKIEL! ZADKIEL!

Archangel Chamuel Prayer

Archangel Chamuel, guardian of Mars and the Church of Pergamos, remove shame and grant me acceptance. CHAMUEL! CHAMUEL! CHAMUEL!

Archangel Haniel Prayer

Archangel Haniel, guardian of Venus and the Church of Thyatira, remove grief and grant me care. HANIEL! HANIEL! HANIEL!

Archangel Raphael Prayer

Archangel Raphael, guardian of Mercury and the Church of Sardis, remove lies and grant me the ability to speak the Truth. RAPHAEL! RAPHAEL! RAPHAEL!

Archangel Gabriel Prayer

Archangel Gabriel, guardian of Luna and the Church of Philadelphia, remove numbness and grant me disillusionment. GABRIEL! GABRIEL! GABRIEL!

Archangel Michael

Archangel Michael, guardian of Sol and the Church of Laodicea, remove from me attachment and grant me objectivity. MICHAEL! MICHAEL! MICHAEL!

Chapter Six: Pleromic Prayers

The Pleromic Prayers are about the forces of the Pleroma. In the Pleroma is the fullness of divinity, the realm of the marvelous beings or Aeons (such as the Logos and Sophia) who make up the highest heaven. It is the highest state of reality and is the ultimate goal of spiritual evolution. The physical universe is seen as a fallen or incomplete state. The purpose of spiritual practice is to return to the Pleroma and achieve unity with the Divine.

Pleroma shows up in the New Testament at least seventeen times in one case or another, fulfilling the explanation I gave above. The only concepts not blatantly spoken about are the Aeons and Jesus and Mary's connection to the Pleroma, at least not directly. This seems to be due to the selective choosing of information on the part of the Nicaean Council. I would imagine they removed this "heresy" because, on the surface, it seems to be a form of polytheism. In reality, it is a form of emanationism.

Emanationism is a metaphysical concept that proposes that all matter and consciousness are derived from a single source. Aspects are seen as arising from a single, ultimate principle through a series of successive "emanations" or outward expressions of the divine (notice how this connects with Kabbalah). In contrast, polytheism is the belief in multiple gods or deities separate and distinct from each other and the universe as a whole.

"The Chymical Wedding of Christian Rosenkreutz" by Johann Valentin Andreae (1616)

Prayer of the Sacred Union

O' Union of unions, Holy Marriage that birthed our Creator who gave us life, You Are Sacred and Awesome. Reveal to us your Gnosis and be with us at the heart of our integration.

Veni Creator Spiritus

Come, Holy Spirit, Creator, blessed,

And in our hearts, take up Your rest.

Come with your Grace and heavenly aid,

To fill the hearts which You have made.

Ein Sof - "Infinite", "Without End"

Emanator's Prayer

Emanator of living Light, shine in us and show us the Way.

Return us to Your Oneness through our fiery hearts and willing hands; make our desires align with Yours.

Give us this day Gnosis and bread, for we are not sustained on bread alone.

Unbind us from our guilt as we unbind others from our blame.

Let us not be forgetful or forgotten, but free us from naivete.

From you came sovereignty, discipline, and the poetic beauty of life that was, is and is to come.

May these words be my nature sealed in trust, faith, and Truth.

Amen.

"Mary Magdalene" meditating on a skull. By Jan Cossiers (1650)

Hail Mary Magdalene

Hail Mary Magdalene, most beloved of the Apostles, Queen of Heaven; Hail Sophia, Mother of us gods ascending bright. Advocate of Grace, watch over us and gift us your prudence.

"Figure of Christ" by Heinrich Hoffman (1884)

The Jesus Prayer

Jesus, have mercy on me, a sinner.
Christ Logos, have mercy on us, Your Church.

Note on the Mysteries In The Following Chapters

The following chapters are the Mysteries. The top of the Mystery chapters shows the name of the Mystery and the correspondence of the Mysteries. The correspondences begin with a planet, a day of the week, a holiday, and a virtue. The likenesses help you choose what mysteries to utilize and when if you desire. This can also help you decide what Mysteries to contemplate during supplication.

Chapter Seven: Mysteries of the Emanator

Planetary Correspondence: Sol

Day Correspondence: Sundays

Holiday Correspondence: Lammas

Virtue Correspondence: Faithfulness

The nature of the Divine or Absolute is often understood to be mysterious and unknowable. The Divine is the source of all things, but it is beyond the comprehension of the human mind. As such, it is impossible to fully understand or comprehend the Divine, and any attempts to do so are ultimately futile. Yet, we try with all of our faith and heart. The mysteries of the Emanator refer to the various aspects of the Divine or Absolute that are unknowable or beyond human understanding. These mysteries include the nature of the Divine, Its role in creation, and the evolution of all things.

Decades

I. **First and Last Mystery (1Pistis Sophia 1:1-2)**

God is the ultimate Mystery and is the last Mystery. As the Mystery of mysteries, we will never know the One's fullness until we are one with God.

II. **The One is Ineffable (Sophia of Jesus 1:5-6)**

God has no end, beginning, discerning attribute, or gender. The Emanator is the great equilibration of all things. We are saved from our ignorance through the Gnosis of Jesus and Mary.

III. **Jesus Rejected by His People (John 10:22-42)**

Although we are not entirely enfolded in the Emanator's Oneness, we are with the One inside and out. We are ourselves, little gods.

IV. **Secrecy and Humility (Matthew 6:5-6)**

The One, who is secret, enjoys secrecy and humility. When we pray or perform rituals, it is an intimate moment with the Most High and not meant to be a boastful act. We do this Work not to gain attention but for our ascension and closeness to God.

V. Trial and Temptation (James 1:12-18)

Although the Emanator is of all things and all abilities, God does not tempt us. We are tempted by our worldly desires and misunderstand our inner darkness. But the Emanator will aid us in freeing ourselves from temptations.

Chapter Eight: Mysteries of Resurrection

Planetary Correspondence: Pluto

Day Correspondence: Sundays

Holiday Correspondence: All Hallows Eve

Virtue Correspondence: Chastity

In many religious traditions, resurrection refers to the belief that the dead will be brought back to life, either in the physical body or in a spiritual form. The mysteries of resurrection refer to the various aspects of this belief that are not fully understood or explained. One of the Mysteries of resurrection is the nature of the afterlife and what happens to the soul. Different religious traditions have different beliefs about the afterlife; what happens to the soul after death is often seen as a mystery.

Another mystery of resurrection is the mechanics of how the dead are brought back to life. Different traditions have different beliefs about this process, and the exact details of how the dead are resurrected are often seen as a mystery. Additionally, the idea of resurrection raises questions about the nature of time and the relationship between the physical world and the spiritual realm. Many religious traditions believe that the dead will be resurrected at some point. However, this event's exact timing and circumstances are often seen as a mystery.

Decades

I. Dying and Rising with Christ (Romans 6:1-14)

We must die in this life to continue living when this body dies. We do this through baptism, self-control, and true chastity.

II. Resurrection of Jesus (Mark 16:1-11)

Even the faithful apostles could not believe that Jesus had mastered the grave until He revealed Himself to them personally. With this confirmation, the hearts of the apostles became chaste.

III. Resurrection Revealed (Treatise on Resurrection 1:10)

We live in the knowledge that we are born again, died, and

risen. Many are insecure about the notion of resurrection. Yet, whether it is a metaphorical or literal statement, it is a truth.

IV. **Lazarus Risen to Life (John 11:1-44)**

We will be risen by our faith and the faith of others. We must be prepared for the day when we are restored in a body of Light or flesh to meet the One who raises us.

V. **The Mission of the Twelve (Matthew 10:5-15)**

We are called to do all the good works of the Lord. One of these is the raising of the dead. What miracles will your chaste heart perform? Will you raise the flesh or a body of Light?

Chapter Nine: Mysteries of Sophia

Planetary Correspondence: Luna

Day Correspondence: Monday

Holiday Correspondence: Full and New Moon

Virtue Correspondence: Self-Control

The Mysteries of Sophia refer to the various aspects of Sophia or Mary Magdalene that are not fully understood or explained. Sophia is half, Logos being the other half, of the second force of the Trinity, alongside God the Father or the Emanator and the Holy Spirit. Sophia, the divine feminine often associated with Wisdom. Lady Sophia is the Divine Mother who played a central role in the world's creation. She is also often associated with mysticism and is revered as a powerful and influential figure within the Pleroma (the Highest Heaven).

Decades

I. **Mary Magdalene Exorcised of Demons (Luke 8:1-5)**

Although Mary Magdalene was the incarnation of Holy Sophia, she had become possessed through the suppression of Her seven lampstands/chakras. While in the flesh and the holiest of us can be owned by our darkness if we cannot fulfill our purpose.

II. **The Thirteenth Apostle (Gospel of Mary 4:21-39)**

Mary reveals the Truth of Christ's nature: He is within us as much as He is outside us. Both sin and our salvation from it come from within.

III. **Most Beloved Among the Apostles (Gospel of Mary 5:1-11)**

Mary proving why she was most beloved and privileged among the apostles, raised the spirits of her brothers. We must be like our Mother Mary Magdalene and lift the heart of our brothers and sisters.

IV. **The Apostles Part Ways (Gospel of Mary 9:1-10)**

Mary faced adversity every step of the way because of Her gender but stayed in control of herself, speaking the Truth. We all should be so wise as the incarnate Wisdom.

V. Gnosis (Thunder, Perfect Mind)

Have no apprehension about the Wisdom poured out to us from the heavenly Pleroma. Be open and willing.

Chapter Ten: Mysteries of Suffering

Planetary Correspondence: Mars & Saturn

Day Correspondence: Tuesday and Saturday

Holiday Correspondence: Spring Equinox and Easter

Virtue Correspondence: Patience

The mysteries of suffering refer to the various aspects of suffering and pain that are not fully understood or explained. These mysteries include the reasons for suffering, the purpose of suffering, and how individuals can cope with and overcome suffering. Exoterically, the Mystery of suffering is linked to the concept of original sin, the belief that humanity is inherently fallen in nature due to the actions of Adam and Eve in the Garden of Eden. According to this belief, suffering is a consequence of original sin and punishment for humanity's disobedience and rebellion against God.

Esoterically, the material world, including the human

body, was created by a corrupt deity known as a Demiurge. Suffering results from being trapped in the material world and subject to the Demiurge's whims. The Mystery of suffering is often seen as a test or a challenge that individuals must overcome to grow spiritually and attain salvation and/or enlightenment. Suffering is an opportunity for individuals to demonstrate their faith and commitment to spiritual growth.

Decades

I. The Work of the Spirit (John 16:1-15)

We suffer not for the sake of it but rather to be ready for the Kingdom, for the sake of our ascension. We will not be welcomed by the world with our message but instead shunned and abused like Jesus.

II. Carrying the Cross (Luke 23:26-31)

We all have our cross to bear. Even when we are suffering from the weight of our inadequacy, we should understand this unites us in understanding with our neighbor.

III. The Crucifixion of Jesus (Luke 23:32-38)

In our suffering and even the death of our bodies, we will be mocked and ridiculed, but we cannot submit to fear and agitation. As a substitute, we should beg God to show mercy to those who do this to the suffering.

IV. **The Letter From James (James 1:1-4)**

We should take our suffering as a test of our willpower and patience. It gives us a chance to see where we need more Work and where we have progressed.

V. **The Beatitudes (Matthew 5:1-12)**

We are blessed by our suffering. When we rise above the urge to wallow in our sorrows, this fills us with fulfillment. The Kingdom is in our grasp.

Chapter Eleven: Mysteries of the Holy Spirit

Planetary Correspondence: Mercury

Day Correspondence: Wednesday

Holiday Correspondence: New Year's Day and Fall Equinox

Virtue Correspondence: Generosity

T he mysteries of the Holy Spirit refer to the various aspects of the Holy Spirit that are not fully understood or explained. The Holy Spirit is the third force of the Trinity, alongside God the Father or the Emanator, and the Sacred Union of Jesus and Mary. The Holy Spirit is often seen as a source of guidance, Wisdom, and divine inspiration. It is believed to be present in the lives of believers. Some Mysteries of the Holy Spirit include the nature and role of the Holy Spirit within the Trinity, how the Holy Spirit communicates with believers, and how the Holy Spirit works in the world. One Mystery of the Holy Spirit is the exact nature of the relationship between the Holy Spirit and the other members of the Trinity.

The Holy Spirit is often closely connected to the Emanator and the Sacred Union. Even so, the precise nature of this relationship is not fully understood or explained. Another mystery of the Holy Spirit is how the Holy Spirit communicates with believers. The Holy Spirit is often seen as a source of guidance and Wisdom. The exact ways this guidance is given are not fully understood. Some believe the Holy Spirit speaks directly to believers through prayer or meditation. In contrast, others believe that the Holy Spirit works through other people or events.

Decades

I. Glorify God in the body (1 Corinthians 6:12-20)

Your body is a temple for the Holy Spirit; with this knowledge, we must discern how we treat the body. A part of being generous allows us to restrict ourselves in ways we could not if we had too much.

II. The Purpose of Parable (Luke 8:9-10)

When we are connected to the Holy Spirit, the Truth of the

higher teachings is revealed. Gnosis is intuitive knowledge given by the Holy Spirit that helps us understand the reality of what is known.

III. **Gifts of the Holy Spirit (Romans 12:6-8, 1Corinthians 12:8-10, 1Peter 4:11)**

The gifts of the Holy Spirit are not just signs of our attainment nor a tool of amusement but are given to us to add to our generosity and ability to help.

IV. **The Descent of the Holy Spirit (Acts 2:1-13)**

The Holy Spirit moves and takes hold so that we may confess to others the Truth of the Kingdom. Through every believer, the Generosity of God is given.

V. **The Commissioning of the Disciples (Matthew 28:16-20)**

Every one of us is a disciple of the Lord. We are meant to spread the message and power of the Holy Spirit to raise our neighbors' consciousness and the Creator Demiurge's into the Pleroma.

Chapter Twelve: Mysteries of the Logos

Planetary Correspondence: Jupiter

Day Correspondence: Thursday

Holiday Correspondence: Winter Solstice & Christmas

Virtue Correspondence: Peace

In many religious traditions, Logos is seen as a fundamental principle or force responsible for the universe's creation and organization. The Mysteries of the Logos refer to the various aspects of this concept that are not fully understood or explained. Logos is often understood as the Word of God or the divine principle of reason and Order in the universe. The Mysteries of the Logos include His nature and role in organizing creation, the relationship between Him and other members of the Trinity, and how He is revealed to humanity. Logos is often seen as a Divine principle of masculinity.

Decades

I. The Annunciation (Luke 1:26-38)

When the time comes, God will call us to a specific mission, and we will have the choice to say 'yes' or 'no.' This is part of being fulfilled. We must say 'yes.' This will bring inner peace.

II. The Three Magi (Matthew 2:1-11)

The three magi could have turned the holy family in for a reward, but they did what was right in the face of evil. What would you do in the face of such evil? We must be brave to be righteous. Bold, honest people bring peace to the world.

III. Baptism of Jesus (Mark 1:1-15)

Fulfilling our life's purpose makes us a tool for peace. When we do what is necessary, we will be rewarded beyond riches.

IV. The Transfiguration (Matthew 17:1-13)

Jesus transfigured into his light body before three of his most trusted disciples to show them a vision of the Pleroma. He did this so that they would seek the peace of being holy. We, too, must pursue this holiness.

V. The Institution of the Eucharist (Luke 22:14-23)

The ultimate peace was given to us in the Eucharist, symbolizing the sacrifice of Jesus. We are called to commune with God and our brothers and sisters.

Chapter Thirteen: Mysteries of Love

Planetary Correspondence: Venus

Day Correspondence: Friday

Holiday Correspondence: May Eve

Virtue Correspondence: Kindness

L ove is a fundamental principle or force present in the universe, and the mysteries of Love refer to the various aspects of this principle that are not fully understood or explained. One of the mysteries of Love is the nature of Love itself. Love is often seen as a complex and multi-faceted emotion or state of being, and the exact nature of Love is not fully understood or explained. This Mystery may include questions about how Love is experienced, how it is expressed, and how it can be nurtured and grown.

Another mystery of Love is the relationship between Love and other spiritual principles or forces. Love is often seen as closely connected to other spiritual principles, such as

Wisdom, compassion, and faith, and the exact nature of this relationship is not fully understood or explained. Finally, the mysteries of Love include how Love is revealed to humanity and how it can be cultivated and nurtured in individuals and communities. Love is often seen as a powerful force that can transform individuals and communities. Even now, the exact ways this transformation occurs are not fully understood or explained.

Decades

I. Truth (Gospel of Philip 1:14)

Truth is Love, and Love is Truth. Truth is a kindness that we share with pure honesty.

II. The Three Marys (Gospel of Philip 1:43)

Mary Magdalene was the companion of Jesus. She was the kindest and most beloved of the apostles.

III. The Gift of Love (1Corinthians 13)

Love is the ultimate gift and power. In fact, of all the powers the Holy Spirit gifts us, Love is supreme. We share Love through care and kindness.

IV. **Good Stewards of God's Grace (1Peter 4:8-10)**

Our Love and kindness towards our neighbor are God's Grace and Love for humanity.

V. **Nicodemus Visits Jesus (John 3:1-21)**

Love is why we were all saved from an ill fate. That without the Love of the Most High, we would have ended up without the ability to be redeemed.

Chapter Fourteen: Mysteries of Light

Planetary Correspondence: Uranus

Day Correspondence: Saturday

Holiday Correspondence: Candlemas

Virtue Correspondence: Joy

L ight is often seen as a fundamental force present within the fabric of the universe. The mysteries of Light refer to the various aspects of this principle that are not fully understood or explained. One of the mysteries of Light is the nature of Light itself. Light is a powerful and transformative force that is present in the fabric of the universe, and the exact nature of this force is not fully described. This Mystery includes questions about how Light is experienced, how it is expressed, and how it can be harnessed and used.

Another mystery of Light is the relationship between Light and other spiritual principles and forces. Light is often seen as being closely connected to love, Wisdom, and Truth, and the exact nature of this relationship is not fully known. The mysteries of Light also include how Light is revealed to humanity and how it can be cultivated and nurtured in individuals and communities.

Decades

I. **The Treasuries of Light (Book of Jeu 42)**

The Light of God transforms all sin. Nothing in this world is irredeemable, but this does not keep us from responsibility for any pain we cause. We must live in the joy that we are forgiven by ourselves and the redeemer.

II. **The Light of the Body (Luke 11:33-36)**

The Light from the Emanator can only enter a healthy body; once we have that Light, it can never be truly hidden. The sensation of the Light within is joy.

III. **Salt and Light (Matthew 5:13-16)**

We are not our bodies, but the body is a container. When the body houses Light, it is a glorious thing that transfigures the spirit.

IV. **God is Light (1 John 1:5-10)**

The Light that enters us and transfigures our spirit is God.

This eliminates all darkness from within, transforming

darkness into a helpful Light that allows us joy in a world of

darkness.

V. **A Vision of Christ (Revelation 1:9-16)**

John's vision of Jesus is faithful proof of eternal life, the joyful

Light Body, and the internal Light illumined by the Emanator.

Chapter Fifteen: Mysteries of Prophecy

Planetary Correspondence: Neptune

Day Correspondence: Saturday

Holiday Correspondence: Summer Solstice

Virtue Correspondence: Modesty

Many have tried to reveal these mysteries repeatedly. In turn, many churches have claimed through history that they lived in the times depicted in Revelations. It is up to us to unlock these scriptures' significance for ourselves. In Truth, Revelations is a coded message about the history of the abuse under the rule of the Roman Empire. The proof of this is in the Gematria. 666 is a numerical cipher for the name of Caesar Nero. Under his reign, Christians suffered immensely. This tragic abuse was the groundwork that prepared the way for Emperor Constantine to deceive the Christians into rejecting the Gnostics, their Christian brothers and sisters.

Decades

I. The Seven-Fold Things (Revelation 2, 3, 5, 6, 8, 9, 10:1-4, 11, 15:1-8, 16:1-17)

II. The Four-Fold Things (Revelation 4:6-11, 7:1-8)

III. The Dragon and His Beasts (Revelation 6:2, 12:1-17, 13:1-18, 16:13-14, 17:1-18, 19:20, 20:1-3)

IV. The Harvests (Revelation 14:14-20)

V. New Heaven and Earth (Revelation 21)

Chapter Sixteen: Alternative Uses of the Holy Reintegrated Rosary

Traditionally in the Church that founded the Rosary, the prayer beads have no alternative use, only being designated for prayer. In other traditions where prayer beads are utilized, the beads are used for more than prayer. With this in mind, the Elders of The Mystical Order of the Nazarene decided it would be appropriate to make a small compilation of the possible alternative uses of the Holy Reintegrated Rosary. Alternative use cases for the HRR are not limited to what is written within this book, so please be creative as possible.

Pendulum

A pendulum is a simple tool used for divination. This practice is said to help individuals gain insight into a question or situation. A pendulum is believed to tap into the subconscious mind and access information that is not readily available to the conscious mind. In some spiritual traditions, the pendulum is seen as a sacred tool that can connect the user to the Divine or a higher power. It is believed to be a conduit through which the user can receive guidance and Wisdom.

To use a pendulum, the user holds it by a chain or string and allows it to hang freely. The user then asks a question and focuses on the answer, allowing the pendulum to swing in response. The pendulum movements are believed to provide information and guidance, with different directions representing different answers or messages. It mostly answers with "yes" or "no" responses and can give us better insights into certain circumstances. Trust your intuition and detach yourself from all possible answers to remain neutral.

Pendulums can pick up the slightest changes in energy and energetic vibrations, so it is best to be entirely in the present when doing divination work and to call on God before divining. When there is positive energy in the environment, in an object, or the answer is yes, it will revolve clockwise. However, if the power is negative in an environment, in an object, or the answer is no, it will circle counterclockwise. Many people who use the pendulum as a divination tool believe it can provide accurate and valuable insights into various questions and situations. It is often used for decision-making, problem-solving, and gaining clarity on difficult or complex issues.

Whether one believes in the power of the pendulum, its use as a tool for divination is an ancient practice still used today.

A Reminder Of Our Spiritual Nature

Wearing the Rosary as a necklace or a bracelet reminds us that we are not just a body but a beautiful, illuminated spirit made of shimmering Light of all colors. Wearing a Rosary can remind us of our spiritual nature, commitment to the Christian faith, and humanity. It can be a visual representation of the individual's devotion to God and their desire to live a life aligned with the teachings of the Logos and Sophia.

Furthermore, wearing the Rosary can serve as a reminder to pray and to keep one's focus on the things of God rather than the distractions and temptations of the world. It can also symbolize unity with the broader community of believers, as the Rosary is a devotion shared by many people worldwide. In short, wearing the Rosary can serve as a powerful reminder of one's spiritual nature and commitment to the Christian faith and can help to keep the individual focused on their relationship with God.

Amulet and Talisman

An amulet is a small object believed to have the power to protect the person who carries it from harm or to bring good luck. A talisman is a similar type of object that is believed to have magical or supernatural powers. Amulets and talismans are often worn or carried by individuals to ward off negative energies or attract positive ones. Like an amulet or talisman, the Rosary is often worn by individuals to protect themselves and bring good luck. It is believed the prayers of the Rosary and contemplations have the power to protect the person who wears it from harm and to bring blessings into their life.

Furthermore, the Rosary is often seen as a robust spiritual growth and transformation tool. It is believed that the repetition of the prayers and the meditations on the mysteries of the Christian faith can help the person who prays the Rosary to grow closer to God and become a better person. In this way, the Rosary can be seen as having similar qualities to an amulet and a talisman in that it is believed to have the power to protect and bring blessings.

Magick Ritual

One way that the Rosary can be used in the magick ritual is to focus the mind and raise energy. The repetitive nature of the prayers and the movement of the beads can help to calm the mind and create a sense of grounding and connection. This can make it easier to enter a meditative state and to raise and direct energy for a specific purpose. Additionally, the Rosary can connect with specific forces or powers. To utilize the Rosary as a tool for casting a magick circle, all one has to do is perform the Rosary while walking in a clockwise circle. When you are done with your ritual, remember to reverse the circle. To do this, walk counterclockwise while performing the Rosary once again.

Sleep Aid

Some people may find that the repetitive nature of the prayers and the soothing sensation of moving the beads can also help aid relaxation and falling asleep. To use the Rosary for sleep, you can simply hold it in your hand and focus on the repetition of the prayers and the movement of the beads. This can help to calm the mind and allow the individual to relax, letting go of any racing thoughts or worries that may be keeping them awake. Additionally, some people may find that focusing on the mysteries of the Christian faith, which are often meditated on during the recitation of the Rosary, can provide a sense of comfort and peace. This can also help to promote relaxation and sleep. In short, the Rosary can be a helpful tool for aiding relaxation and falling asleep due to its repetitive nature and association with spiritual reflection and meditation.

Blessing Your Home

To bless your home, you first need to cleanse the space by sprinkling holy water in each room, starting at the front door and moving clockwise throughout the house. As you sprinkle the water, you can recite a prayer or phrase asking for God's blessings and protection over the home and its inhabitants.

Next, you would use the Rosary to pray for specific blessings for the home and its inhabitants. For example, you could pray the Rosary and meditate on the mysteries of the Rosary, asking for God's Grace and guidance in the lives of those who live in the home. You could also pray specific prayers, such as the "Hail Mary Magdalene" or "The Emanator's Prayer," asking for God's protection and blessings on the home and its inhabitants.

It is important to remember that blessing home with holy water and a Rosary is a sacred and symbolic act. It should be done with reverence and intention. The power of the blessing comes from the faith and devotion of the person performing it, not the objects themselves.

Chapter Seventeen: Rite of Holy Water

After adding the suggestion of blessing your home it seemed only appropriate to provide an operation for Holy Water. Holy water is water that has been blessed by a member of the clergy or a religious figure. It is used in various religious rituals to purify or sanctify objects or people. In many cultures and religions, holy water is believed to have special powers. It is used for a variety of purposes.

In Gnostic Christianity, holy water is used in several different ways. It may be used in baptism ceremonies, where it is poured over the head of the person being baptized to cleanse them of sin and make them a church member. In some Gnostic traditions, holy water is also used in healing rituals, where it is believed to have the power to cure illness and disease.

The use of holy water is not unique to Gnostic Christianity, however. It has been a part of many different cultures and religions throughout history. In ancient Egyptian religion, for example, water was considered to be a sacred substance and was often used in purification rituals. In Hinduism, water is also considered to be a purifying substance and is used in a variety of religious ceremonies.

In the Catholic Church, holy water is used in many different ways. It is commonly used in baptism ceremonies, where it is poured over the head of the baptized person. It is also used to bless objects and places, such as homes, churches, and cemeteries. In some Catholic traditions, holy water is also used in the exorcism of demons and other evil spirits. Within the Catholic Church clergy only has the power to consecrate water for these purposes.

The use of the Holy Water in the Christian and Judaic traditions is said to come from Numbers 5:17, "the priest shall take holy water in an earthen vessel and take some of the dust that is on the floor of the tabernacle and put it into the water." The ritual of making Holy Water presented is based on this scripture. The only difference is that in the tradition of The Mystical Order of the Nazarene, a Gnostic Christian tradition, we recognize that being One and with Christ makes us all priests and priestesses.

Supplies

† Purified Warm Water

† Organic Salt

† Stirring Utensil

† Two Bowls

† A Vessel for the Holy Water

† Incense

Procedure

Declare your intention as you see fit or make this declaration:

"I come before the earthly spirits, the angels, Holy Spirit, the Son the Messiah, and Our Father the Lord of the Universe to purify these gifts of water and salt and empower them with Light. I do this out of Agape and the need for the intervention of the Most High. Before all this is high and low, this rite begins! Ephphatha! The temple is open!"

Take your incense banish and consecrate each side of your working space moving clockwise:

"In the East, I banish all beings of the air that are vile and malignant wishing to interrupt this Work and may Light only enter herein. (Stomp your left foot.)

In the South, I banish all beings of fire that are vile and malignant wishing to interrupt this Work and may Light only enter herein. (Stomp your left foot.)

In the West, I banish all beings of water that are vile and malignant wishing to interrupt this Work and may Light only enter herein. (Stomp your left foot.)

In the East, I banish all beings of earth that are vile and malignant wishing to interrupt this Work and may Light only enter herein. (Stomp your left foot)."

Now back in the western part of your space facing

East bow your head with hands in the sign of prayer, hands

pointing up walk around your work altar 9 times clockwise

while saying:

"Holy, holy, holy, Lord God Almighty, which was, and is, and is to come!"

Now facing the East, recite the "Adoration to the

Holy Ternion."

Now evoke the Holy Spirit:

"O' Most Holy Spirit, from you all of man may know the wisdom of the Lord. Come, I humbly pray. Come and witness this rite. Be my benefactor in this holy Work and find joy in it. I humbly ask You, Most Clean Spirit, with the Love of Christ residing within my heart. Come down from your heavenly abode and radiate your Grace upon me within this circle. Amen. Amen. Amen."

In separate bowls, place the salt and water. Hover

your hands above the salt while reciting this exorcism (vibrate

the names in all caps):

"The blessing of ABBA SHADDAI be upon this creature of
salt and let all corruption and hindrance be cast-out
henceforth, and let Lux enter herein; for without You man
cannot live, and You formed man from this humble element. I
bless and evoke GIBOR ADONAI that You may aid me.
AMEN."

Cross the salt as you vibrate, 'AMEN.'

Now with your hands hovering over the water, recite

this exorcism (vibrating all names in caps again):

"I exorcise you, creature of water, by YOD HE VAU HE Who
created you and gathered you together into one place so that
the dry land appeared, that you may uncover all the deceits of
the enemy and He cast out from you all the impurities and the
uncleanliness of the Spirits of the World of Phantasm, so you
may harm none, through the Virtue of EL SHADDAI, His Son
YAHOSHUA, and RUACH HAKODESH; Who reigns
forevermore,

AMEN."

Cross the water as you vibrate. "AMEN."

Pour the exorcised salt into the exorcised water.

Calling down the Light of the Spirit, stir the mixture clockwise

while reciting Psalm 118:14-24 (no vibration):

"The LORD is my strength and my song;

he has given me victory.

Songs of joy and victory are sung in the camp of the godly.

The strong right arm of the LORD has done glorious things!

The strong right arm of the LORD is raised in triumph.

The strong right arm of the LORD has done glorious things!

I will not die; instead, I will live

to tell what the LORD has done.

The LORD has punished me severely,

but he did not let me die.

Open for me the gates where the righteous enter,

and I will go in and thank the LORD.

These gates lead to the presence of the LORD,

and the godly enter there.

I thank you for answering my prayer

and giving me victory!

The stone that the builders rejected

has now become the cornerstone.

This is the LORD's doing,

and it is wonderful to see.

This is the day the LORD has made.

We will rejoice and be glad in it."

When the salt is mainly dissolved, pour it into the chosen vessel, hover your hands over it, and recite "The Emanaor's Prayer." As you say, "Amen," cross the salt water.

Take the now Holy Water going in a clockwise motion starting in the East, consecrating your space once again:

"Blessings in the East may all goodly spirits of air enter herein.

Blessings in the South may all goodly spirits of fire enter herein.

Blessings in the West may all goodly spirits of water enter herein.

Blessings in the North may all goodly spirits of earth enter herein."

Return to the western part of your space and place the Holy Water on the altar. Walk around the altar counter-clockwise nine times, head bowed with hands in prayer:

"Holy, holy, holy, Lord God Almighty, which was, and is, and is to come!"

Now facing the East, reciting the "Adoration to the Holy Ternion."

License the Holy Spirit's departure,

"Most Gracious Paraclete, in You I lay my trust and faith. You are everywhere and ever pervading, but my Work here is done. May Your Presence be with me always, but I no longer need You for now, and may You favor me in my time of need. Baruch Ha'Shem. Amen. Amen. Amen."

Now declare that the ritual is over in your own way, or recite this:

"My ritual is now done to all beings above and below, to the North, East, South, and West. My circle has been undone in the right manner. I have fulfilled my will, and all doors are closed. So be it done! Ha'Mashalam! The temple is closed!"

Now you can utilize the Holy Water for whatever purpose you deem appropriate. The salt will help the water keep from stagnating, but it is best to refresh the vessel every three months or less. Be sure not to dump the water into the grass, flower beds, or any other garden. Saltwater will kill any plant and could keep anything else from growing there for a while.

Chapter Eighteen: Keepers of the Rose Tree

Every man and woman have it within themselves to be more than what they were made to believe they are. Reinventing ourselves begins with sitting down, learning ourselves, understanding God, and coming into the Heart of Grace through meditation (Psalm 46:10). Not to perfect ourselves or to become superior to another. Instead, we should strive to be better than who we were yesterday – regardless of the struggle around us. Easier said than done, I understand. It is a process. No one wakes up one day, and life's ills are less burdensome. No, it is a cycle of failing to understand a lesson life throws and revisiting it at unlikely times until we learn.

Wherever we are in life, we all need reorientation and refocusing from time to time. Maybe daily? Taking a few moments to focus on the breath will allow us to be more aware of our actions and how those actions are the catalyst to the kind of life we are living. We can blame so many people, our circumstances, or how we were treated at one point or another, but it is up to us to be that change. It is up to us to break that cycle of pain by committing to be a representative of God's Divine Love, Agape.

This does not mean to make ourselves complete pacifists. It is an ancient wisdom that we should understand that too much mercy is weakness and too much severity is cruelty. We must walk this fine line, which comes from a nonaggression principle that allows you to defend your life. The base meaning of "blessed is he who has crucified the world, and who has not allowed the world to crucify him."[1]

It is daunting to want more for ourselves; most just do not know where to begin. That is the mission of this book. To guide those who need it so you can eventually make your own way when ready. The point of any tradition is to raise us up spiritually self-sufficient and a tool to teach the next generation the Way.

How could anyone know where to begin on their own? We are lied to on so many levels. When we go to

---

[1] Krause, Robinson, Wisse, et al., "Frist Book of Jeu", *The Coptic Gnostic Library* (1978), p. 44

churches looking for guidance, most priests and ministers leave us even more confused than before we came to them for help. I cannot blame all clergy, at least most. They are stuck in the false paradigms they grew up with, which has helped them to a degree. However, they are stuck in a tradition of avoiding the Truth and neglecting the Rose Tree.

The Rose Tree is a sign of enlightenment, a sign of power, a sign of Love, and, ultimately, a true sign of the Christian tradition. The Tree only began to wither because of the pruning of the Nicaean Council. Leaving enough foliage to keep the Tree alive but too little to sustain the institution into this age, this age thirsty for Truth. We have the Truth in our hands and hearts. To reveal it, we must make the eye single – we must open our spiritual eyes.

When you walk away from this book, even if you do not believe in the Sacred Union of Jesus and Mary Magdalene, there are two things I hope you learned: the Truth is much more complicated, and we need to at least train our minds to have a better life. The Holy Reintegrated Rosary will do this and so much more. Even if you broke down the Rosary for its technical parts, you would still come away with a meditative practice that will enhance and enrichen your life. With that said, the power and Love that radiates from the Truth revealed in the HRR is beyond secular meditation.

When we give ourselves to God, we open ourselves to an incomprehensible torrent of power and Love. We can meditate and meditate as much as we want. Unfortunately, suppose we do not eventually contemplate the Divine. In that case, we have left again with that hollow feeling, usually filled with delusional arrogance. This is another symptom of the times. A sign of the lies.

It is no coincidence or accident that we build stories from the same archetypes, that religions share a deific similarity. The same symbols that make up that dream are found cross-culturally when we dream. This all means something, and that meaning is the profound connection of consciousness. This may not be God, but it is undeniable proof that there is something beyond us. The fact that we are not happy with our mindless watching of the television and compulsive eating means something. We seek meaning in the things we buy and the clothes we wear just to feel numb – the fact that incessant consuming with little introspection leaves us hollow means something. We seek meaning, and that is not found in an object, not even this Rosary.

The faith of the mustard seed moves the mountain, not the staff. Within us is all the meaning we will ever need; that is where the Kingdom is. Sometimes objects can amplify our faith, but faith alone mobilizes the mystical happening. It is the person who reaches their hand up to God that allows His hand to touch down. This is what makes miracles possible – the power of theurgy.

We seek closeness to God. The meaning we seek is in God - whatever that translates to for you. I will make this abundantly clear, nothing is a coincidence, and there is a reason why you picked up this book. Jesus and Mary Magdalene have made way for you. You have been called on to be a keeper of this Rose Tree. People were made to believe they were far from God and needed an Earthly mediator – another lie. You can come into communion with the One by conviction and faith.

We cannot change the past. Nor should we try to take down institutions we are unprepared to replace. We should not hope to destroy any establishment; instead, we should seek to speak the Truth and unbind people from lies that keep these corrupt organizations in power. We are all keepers of that Rose Tree. A single person or institution cannot be responsible for keeping this garden healthy and fresh.

To my fellow Christians, if this book enrages you, know that is not the point of this book. I want no harm to anyone and do not wish to pull you away from how you practice your faith. I cannot help what I see. I cannot help what I know. I cannot help that the Holy Spirit moved me to write this book. Would you ignore the beckoning of the Lord's call? All I ask from you, my brothers and sisters, is an open mind and heart.

We are called as Christians to "take no part in the unfruitful works of darkness; rather, expose them" (Ephesians 5:11). That is only what I wish to do. It is unfortunate that I must point to the history of the faith as a source of this dark corruption, but this is also something to celebrate. Every sin uprooted brings us closer to the Truth, Love, and God. Should we not strive to be closer to a holier understanding of the faith?

Some would argue that we would bring darkness to others and ourselves. We are misguided in the pursuit of knowing God and living in the Truth. Indeed, this is a statement of fear. These are the words of someone afraid to be cast out from their dead churches and shunned by their loved ones. To them, I would say look at the bloody history of the Roman church and remember that even Jesus and the apostles left their families to speak the Truth. Fear not and live in the Light of Love and Truth.

I will leave you with this verse and pray that the Lord blesses you and keeps you for all time, "For this is the message you have heard from the beginning, that we should love one another. We must not be like Cain, who was from the evil one and murdered his brother. And why did he murder him? Because his own deeds were evil and his brother's righteous. Do not be astonished, brothers and sisters, that the world hates you. We know that we have passed from death to life because we love the brothers and sisters. Whoever does not love abides in death. All who hate a brother or sister are murderers, and you know that murderers do not have eternal life abiding in them" (1John 3:11-15).